the rules of paradise

the rules of paradise

d. nurkse

four way books

**marshfield, vermont
new york, new york**

Editorial Office
Four Way Books
PO Box 535, Village Station
New York, NY 10014
www.fourwaybooks.com

Library of Congress
Catalog Card Number: 00 134374

ISBN 1-884800-38-6

Cover Art: Giovanni Ragusa, *Polvere di stelle*
Property of Credito Valtellinese, Sondrio
Book Design: Brunel

This book is manufactured in the United States of America and
printed on acid-free paper.

Four Way Books is a division of Friends of Writers, Inc.,
a Vermont-based not-for-profit organization. We are
grateful for the assistance we receive from individual donors
and private foundations.

Publication of this book was supported by a generous contribution
from The CIRE Fund.

ACKNOWLEDGMENTS

The American Poetry Review	Written in Dust, San Isidro, Immense Fires and Not Yet Summer
Ascent	The Garden at St Mary's
Barrow Street	Snapshot from Niagara
Cottonwood	August Horizon (published under the title "August at Black River")
Creeping Bent	The Portrait
Footwork	The Hush
Folio	The Latch
Hanging Loose	The Screen, The Invisible Faction, The Last Night of Exile (second section, originally published as "Newborn"), Transience, Rosewood Handles
The Harvard Review	Black River
The Hudson Review	Crossing the Ark Mountains, Rendezvous in Providence
The Kenyon Review	Excelsior Fashion Products, Easter, Scattering the March, Threshold of Liberty
The Manhattan Review	Evening Practice, The Last Night of Exile (first section), Childhood and the Great War, The Book of Loneliness, Childhood and the Great Cities, Prades (published under the title "Anvira"), Olmos, Lake Huron, Plums
The Massachusetts Review	The Master Surgeon
Mss.	The First House
North Dakota Quarterly	Night Walk in Prades (published under the title "Night Walk in Binney's Wood")
Phoebe	Involuntary Music
Pivot	Leaving Black River, The Opponent
Poetry	Introit & Fugue, First Grade Homework, Only Child (© the Modern Poetry Association)
Prairie Schooner	The Birth Room
The Quarterly	The Thread of the Conversation, The Hotel Metropole, The Bond, The Last Night of Fever
Stand (U.K.)	Bushwick, Latex Flat

Willow Springs	Returning to the Capital,
	Fever in a Rented Room, Draft Hall
West Branch	The Next World
The Yale Review	My Father at Prades
Yellow Silk	Evergreen In Summer

Thanks to Milkweed Editions for permission to reprint "Involuntary Music" from *Mixed Voices,* and for permission to reprint "Olmos" from *The Outsider.* Thanks also to Margaret McElberry Books/Simon & Schuster for permission to reprint "Involuntary Music" from *Calling Down The Moon.* "Evergreen in Summer" appeared in *The Book Of Eros* from Crown/Harmony Books, New York. Thanks to Four Way Books for permission to reprint "Bushwick: Latex Flat" from *The Four Way Reader #1.*

"Only Child" was included in the *Poetry Breaks* series, produced by WGBH, Boston, and distributed by the Public Broadcasting Service.

"Little Falls" was reprinted as Number Seven in the Winter Poetry Broadside series, Friends of Kent State University Libraries, under the title "Black River."

"The Master Surgeon" appeared on the National Endowment for the Arts Web Page.

The author is grateful for two fellowships from the National Endowment for the Arts, which allowed many of these poems to be written; for the generous support of the Mrs. Giles Whiting Foundation; for a poetry fellowship from the New York Foundation for the Arts; for an Artist's Fund grant from NYFA; and for a Tanne Foundation grant. Thanks also to the MacDowell Colony, Blue Mountain Center, Yaddo, and the Virginia Center for the Creative Arts.

My gratitude to Howard Stein, Anneliese Wagner, Hal Sirowitz, Gerald Freund, and Marc Kaminsky.

Special thanks to Martha Rhodes for her invaluable close reading.

This book is for Sonia.

CONTENTS

PART ONE

PART TWO

A long war disturbed your mind;
Here your perfect peace is signed.

—John Webster

PART ONE

OLMOS

A man walks a dusty road
dragging a suitcase.
Sometimes he looks back
and sees a shallow rut
wavering beside his footprints.
A dog howls behind a fence.
The man stops and says: shush.
The dog shuts up.
It has never heard such longing.
Olmos: the first border village.
The guards are sitting on barrels,
playing with creased cards.
My father has brought them
grandmother's lace, a pocket watch,
the locket with the child's tresses,
the diary locked with a gold key.
The visors evaluate these souvenirs
with one eye on their cards.
Olmos: a cider mill,
a tavern, a few porches.
A girl on a swing
watches my father
severely from several heights.
Suddenly she scuffs her heels
and runs through a red gate.
A man comes out—a real father—
and stares at the stranger
and spits: Nothing,
and shouts back at the cinched curtain:
Nothing to be afraid of.
Through the half-shut kitchen door

the smell of bread
reaches like a hand
that will mould me out of ashes.

CHILDHOOD AND THE GREAT CITIES

In the dim room, my father
unpacks his books
, and sets them on the dusty shelf
in order of weight.
Marx. The Bible. The Atlas.

He runs a finger
along his knife-edge crease
and coaxes his trousers
into the clasp hanger.
He will not wake me.

These sheets are stiff
from honeymoon come.
I turn to face the wall.
Lovers moan inside the plaster.

Now my father lies beside me
and folds his hands
over his pale belly.
In case I can read his mind,
he dreams in his own language.

*

We are still in the middle of the journey
from Alpha to Omega,
Petersburg to Los Angeles,
worker's state to Kingdom of God.

Each city is larger than the last,

each room smaller,
each keyhole more dazzling.

I tiptoe to the curtain
and see a general on a stone horse,
and moonlit slums—roofs crisscrossed
by immense names, massed laundry,
towers where every window is lit.

After midnight my father grunts
softly, not to wake me.
Soon he begins talking
in the old language,
haltingly at first,
then in a flood
as tears come back to him.

And I'll sit cross-legged until dawn
to guard him from that stranger
with whom he bargains
in a terrified voice.

CHILDHOOD AND THE LAST WAR

It was being fought in another country,
perhaps another continent.
My father said it could not reach us
except as news—the days were headlines,
letters, telegrams, once a voice
crying in the stillness of the hall.

At twilight my father
ran his fingers through my hair
and told me the count of the dead
as if it were my right to know,
as if that knowledge conferred a power
he could not deny me.

How could I sleep?
The room seemed to swell with light
until I lay in a bed
tucked inside the eye.

My father sighed
and fetched me colder water
without being asked.

He shifted from foot to foot,
not daring to leave
while I faked sleep so coyly.

He whispered the great battles:
Verdun, Thermopylae, Cannae.
And the names of the heroes:
Patton, Achilles.

It would be forever until dark.
In the street, older children
were just beginning to play,
their voices raised in jubilant whoops.
A carousel was grinding out a melody
too slow even to be sad.

I peeked through my eyelashes:
the scallops in the wallpaper,
not just watched but watching back
with a harrowing attention.

My bear with four holes
in its button eyes.

The motes of dust orbiting
in the shaft between the curtains,
each more precious than a world.

LAKE HURON

Ashamed of the worm's pain
my father casts
deep into rushes.
Immediately the line quickens
as if it were living—
as if the space
between us were immortal—
and the fish is at our feet.
My father would like to throw it back

to that unreal opposite shore
made of dusk and the color blue
but he can't work the hook
free of the tiny jaw
without causing great harm
perhaps only he can feel

and I watch him grow old
caught in the trance
of a man undoing a knot.
The trout died between us
but its tail still lashes
in a perfect circle—

flesh that was to be our sacrament,
that we were to carry home
for a woman to clean
in one of those lit windows
that have already begun to appear
at intervals along the coast
and also shining from the void.

INVOLUNTARY MUSIC

I practiced the piano all afternoon
while the others played ball.
As I memorized the notes
stepping out of my mind
in time, each harmony
abolishing the one before,
a bat cracked in the distance,
a hitter squealed in delight.
I climbed the ladder of the minor scale
broken at the third and seventh rung,
tucking my thumb under my middle finger
and scuttling up: once, my hand
traveled off the keys and paced
mechanically over black walnut casing
and dropped, and I came to silence:
very far away, I half-heard
the triple-wound metronome
and the scuff of bases being dragged home.

EVENING PRACTICE

I asked my father,
"would you rather die
of cancer or a heart attack?
Would you rather be executed
or put in jail for life?
Which would you rather be—
a spy or a sentinel?"
And he tried to answer
honestly, combing his thinning hair
with his fingers, thinking of something else.
At last he fell silent. I ran out
to savor the dregs of dusk
playing with my friends
in the road that led to the highway.
The ball flew up toward day
and landed in night.
We chanted. Every other minute
a truck, summoned by our warnings,
brushed past in a gust of light,
the driver's curses muffled
by distance: the oncoming wheels
were the point of the game,
like the scores in chalk
or the blood from scuffed knees
that we smeared across our faces:
so when my mother called,
her voice was quaint and stymied
and I took all the time in the world
trotting home past tarped barbecue pits,
past names of lovers filling with sap,
past tentative wind from sprinklers:

then I was stunned to see my golden window
where all faces, hanging plants, dangling pots
were framed by night and dwarfed
by a ravenous inward-turning light.

THE BOOK OF LONELINESS

Each night in the leather-backed chair
my father thumbs the gold-flecked pages.
I peek over his shoulder:
the letters are blurred
with spiky curlicues
—Hebrew or Greek?,
the words seem to quiver
of their own accord.

Put it down, put it down!
Come play with me
in the new-fallen snow.
Your huge boot
will cave my footprints in
until no one can find me.

Or let me sit on your knee
while you tell me stories
of the war long ago—
among the million enemies
wasn't there one you killed?

But my father's eyes
never stray from the page.
At bedtime he just points
to the tall black clock.

And as I lie alone
in that dark room
he will come kiss me
and sing me the lullaby

in a small scared voice,
as if it were his secret
that I'll never see him again.

THE GARDEN AT ST. MARY'S

My grandmother strapped
to her bed explains
the rules of paradise
are that you must have nothing.
She gives me the key
to the ironbound box of jewels
and tells me, "Scatter them
on the clinic grounds."
Wincing at her blue lips,
I ask, "You're going to paradise?"
And she says: "Yes.
Scatter what was mine."
I take the box and creep
down the dusty path
where the gardener won't see me
dropping rubies like seeds:
even as a child I'm certain
they're only tinted glass,
but when I scamper
up the marble steps my father
is waiting with folded arms,
his face white as a sail.

THE NEXT WORLD

I dreamt my father was dead.
I woke and he sat beside me,
reading a book. I watched
through half-closed eyes
while he frowned at one page,
yawned at the next, rubbed his nose,
shuffled out. I heard the fierce stream
of his piss and he tiptoed back
and brushed away a fly settled
in an incised gold letter:

I dreamt my father was hugging me,
when I woke he was dead,
the coffin had already been sealed,
the carpenters were spitting on their hands,
passing around a jar of black wine.
I begged to see his face
but the foreman said: "It's late.
Rub your hands along the grain
and see how it's sanded
glass-smooth: touch the joints
and you won't be able to feel
the seam where the choice mahogany
is spliced to leftover pine."

THE HUSH

The wind blew my father's hair
flat against the creases of his temple
and fluttered his eyelashes.
The coffin was filling
with torn-off petals
but the novices closed it,
staggering as if at sea
toward the hole.
The wind took the preacher's words.
I lip-read Ashes to Ashes, but that
was the one phrase I'd foreseen:
sometimes he licked his finger
and jabbed it among the whipping pages.
Then I fell on my knees and prayed
while the wind pushed its way
between my lips and past my tongue,
shoving breath in my belly.
I whispered, God, God, and in my mind
my voice shouted: but by nightfall
the hush had come. At last I heard
my brother fidgeting in sleep,
the apples in the orchard about to drop,
the cornhusks rubbing together
on the surface of a stream
and a cat's breath.
My mother cried in the parlor
and the old woman who was the mourner
consoled her, wound the clock,
took a break, limped to the porch,
struck a match, blew smoke,
and whispered to herself: Too quiet.
Too quiet. Something will happen.

PRADES

My father's steps
rustle on the stoop.
My mother said he was dead
but she was wrong about the parcel
covered with flower stamps, and wrong
about the trip to Prades
that I wanted so much
I cried until my voice
terrified me. It's his hand
on the door, if there's still a door.
His cough in the hall.
His fingers running through my hair.
His lips on my forehead.
His silence. His terrible tiredness.
His cat watches with hard eyes.
He has brought me chocolate,
even just before supper,
and a snapshot of Prades.
That village. That mountain. That smoke.
And an arrow and a circle
showing the place his body was found.

INTROIT & FUGUE

After death, my father
practices meticulously
until the Bach is seamless,
spun glass in a dream,
you can no longer tell
where the modulations are,
or the pedal shifts
or the split fingerings . . .

if he rests
it's to wind the metronome
or sip his cup of ice . . .

but who is the other old man
in the identical flannel gown,
head cocked, listening
ever more critically,
deeper in the empty room?

MY FATHER AT PRADES

He has left his life
with his baggage in the village.

Now he walks by himself
in the forest at Prades.

A tiny sparrow with a fat chest
hops up and considers him
gravely: he's no longer the enemy.

Under a clump of white mushrooms
no one will harvest
he finds flowers with no names:
a teardrop, a bead of blood.

He stumbles on a hidden spring
and sips a loud rushing voice
and the cold of another planet.

Now he can enter the wild hives
and scoop that cloudy honey
in both hands

and the one who was stung
was a stranger, an exile.

No war, no child, no suffering.

Only the waterfall in the fog.

PART TWO

WE BELIEVED IN THE END OF THE WORLD

We scrunched under the desk
where I once memorized
the lives of saints and heroes

while the teacher droned on
trying to stay calm
in the face of a bomb
that might never fall.

In that rich dark
we learned how we fitted
boy and girl,
how we were our opposites
and each our own opposite.

Above us the stashed gum
of a generation of older brothers
glinted, amazingly hard:
if we tried to carve a heart
that dark sheen cracked.

We believed this world would end:

like water from the fountain
held in cupped hands,
like chalk dust or the powder
from a jelly donut.

Far away the principal rumbled
on his scratchy intercom,

then nothing, the powerful swish
of traffic, silence, time passing,

the pulse quickening
as if to find a way out

and no world except us.

DRAFT HALL

This room once housed heavy machinery.
You can see the bolt-marks on the walls
and the ruts on the carpet.
Now we're huddled here,
a company of naked men.
We've waited for this all morning
but for a few minutes we're shy,
then we piss—streams crisscrossing,
red with sulphur, black with blood,
white with anemia, gold,
then splashing in a variety of dishes,
trays, jam jars, mugs:
now the I who expected a clean test tube
with a name and number
fades into the past,
and the I who expected nothing
stumbles onto the platform scale
in the pack of conscripts
with the needle on the gauge at zero.

THRESHOLD OF LIBERTY

When our eyes met
at the Panther rally
we knew we'd be lovers
for life: now in the narrow room
without that chant roaring
UNITY, we feel spurious,
perhaps we're informers,
perhaps we're junkies.
It's a bleak neighborhood,
transient. In the street
voices of children keep score
with a cold mounting anger.
Tenants in other rooms argue
over the cost of wine or smoke.
We sit on the edge of the bed
and remind each other in whispers
behind every door is the State.

THE INVISIBLE FACTION

White puffs of smoke
at the edge of a demonstration.
We've fallen into the ranks
of the provocateurs, who look like us
but a little more so: newer shoes,
jeans a little more ragged,
eyes harder: sometimes a beard
wobbles on a chin:
they chant as we do
Peace, Peace, but with tighter discipline
and suddenly—as if there were no signal—
the bricks begin raining,
lobbed over us gracefully
into the police ranks
        and we duck into a store
and begin to negotiate:
we've come to purchase a thread
almost green, almost gray
to match a tear
in mother's silk kerchief
—while behind us the street
shakes with the thunder of hooves.

SCATTERING THE MARCH

I was not beaten
but the boy beside me was.
He broke stride, stumbled,
the sticks circled over him,
corralling him into their world.
I met his eyes and lip-read
"run," a whisper
engulfed in sirens.
    I slowed down
in an unknown neighborhood,
a street of watch repairers,
tinsmiths, tailors sitting
cross-legged in dim windows
staring at lacquered Singers
like men whose eyes
are lost in a fire,
and I ducked past them
glancing sideways
in deep pity because I'd been
a step away from freedom.

TRANSIENCE

Foley invited me to spend one night
in his apartment in Shell Gardens.
He said not to look at his wife
or he'd kill me.
We'd met at the Ark Tower site
where I was casual labor,
bundling scraps of steel cable.
He told me he'd once been hungry
in Arkansas with no friends.
He settled me on his sofa
with a shower curtain tacked around me.
All I saw of his wife
was a blur in a housedress.
All night they played cards
in a sweet cloud of hash,
his voice growing slower and louder.
I imagined a slap.
Later they made love.
Lying desperate to piss,
I imagined her moans were for me.
In the black window
the Clark Ridge Skyway
glittered with stalled cars
like white-back grubs.
How I longed to be at that exit
with my cardboard sign saying
COAST, but I had no key
to lock the door behind me.

SAN ISIDRO

On a bridge over the Pace Freeway
a junkie held a knife to my throat
and said: your coat has many pockets.
I took it off very slowly,
the cars passing under me.
I was sure nothing could go wrong
while I was trying to help.
His voice was slurred
as if by great distance
but the blade was steady.
I began telling him a story:
I'd hitchhiked from Pueblo to Cheyenne
looking for work, and found a job
painting the white lines in the road.
The blade pricked against my adam's apple.
I thought: if you're telling this,
you must live through it.
Somewhere a cricket fell silent.
The bridge rocked constantly.
He held the jacket between his legs,
extracted the billfold with one hand,
counted the money with a sidelong glance.
He nodded, as if there were a sum
I owed him, and moved back a step
to let me pass. Then I feared him:
I was no longer entirely at his mercy.
I waited. Traffic passed.
Snatches of music faded.
I said I was waiting for a friend
who would meet me at dawn.
He answered: there is no one,

but he'd begun to back away
with the coat under his arm,
ten steps between us, twenty,
and I was on the other side:
street of shops that seemed miniature,
lamps still lit in daylight.
In front of a shuttered grocery
someone had left hampers of milk and bread.
The silence was absolute.
On the grate of a cantina
signs announced last year's dances.
The gaunt dogs, that sniffed as they pleased,
flinched at my shadow, then caught my scent
and knew I had no power to hurt.
I walked through them as if on stilts.
I came to a phone and dialed.
A holding voice and music.
Another number; another voice, music.
With no more change, I glanced behind me,
and walked quickly past tiny houses.
Toast was burning. A child sobbed.
A sprinkler winced, despite the drought.
A tame dog rattled its chain
and cleared its throat to bark.
I broke into a run. Already
I could hear the hum of the next huge road.

WRITTEN IN DUST

We met on the Trailways
at night in Toledo and rode
to the end of the line
and I watched her walk away
among the miners' manicured lawns
where sprinklers made a soft patter
like bees: the name of that little town
was carved on a slag heap in huge letters
whose surface hovered in the dawn wind.

SNAPSHOT FROM NIAGARA

We'd been married nine days,
the war had lasted a year,
we'd come to the falls
to photograph each other
with that roar behind us—

at dusk we asked an old man
to take a picture of us
embracing, but not too much—

how he fussed with the lenses
while we fumed: now, now,
while there's still light . . .

Already we resented each other
because we'd make us die
while alone we were immortal
like starlight or the breeze

and we were ashamed
never to have thanked him—
to be more lonely than ever
with a sheaf of glossy prints
of two dim faces, woman, man,
worn identical by happiness.

ROSEWOOD HANDLES

I ran through the streets before dawn.
Men were seated around fires.
A few transvestites waited in doorways.
There were signs for sales on the steel grates.
I caught the freight elevator at Pyramid,
punched in, turned on the buffing wheel.
It was a blur with pockets of force;
if a frame caught, the current kicked back.
Sometimes I'd push in a stick of wax
and watch it dissolve, and the air turn orange.
With my left hand, I picked up the frames
Xacuma brought. Occasionally one charred
under friction; the smoke was poison.
Soon I made them glitter like knives.
Almost always, nothing happened.
The armature of the fire escape in the window
slowly filled with snow. In the corner of my eye
a gesture repeated itself, as if to find its flaw.
I heard the different pitches of the drill press,
band saw, router, and the familiar voices
in Spanish or Slovak, discussing birth,
marriage, rosewood frames. Five minutes early
we left, allowed to wash on company time:
the square camphor soap was free.
I drifted home through empty streets.
Sometimes a group of drunks sang rounds
or a man in a suit vest preached the Gospels.
I felt a great wind pushing me.
I paused outside our lobby.
If the light was still on I kept walking
past extrusion mills and die works.

If the light was out I tiptoed upstairs
holding my breath and lay beside you,
squeezing my eyes shut,
training myself to darkness
so I might wake and see your face.

EXCELSIOR FASHION PRODUCTS, EASTER

They pay us time and a half
and don't dare catch us
drinking: we don't insist,
don't pass a bottle, but each sips
a private pint, all sitting
in the narrow room with our backs
to the center, each facing
his work—router, stain tray,
buffing wheel, drill press—
and with that sweet taste echoing
in our bones, we watch our hands
make what they always made
—rosewood handles—but now
we smile in delighted surprise
and Marchesi brings envelopes
that record a full day's work
though it's still noon,
processions still fill the streets,
choirs, loudspeakers bellowing
Hallelujah: and we change
into our finest clothes in the locker room,
admiring each other's hat brims, passing bottles
freely until all are empty, and at last
we separate in the brilliant street, each
in the direction of a different tolling bell.

THE FIRST HOUSE

The sparrows drunk on juniper
fell down the chimney
and their wings turned to fire—

it was the first spring
of our marriage, in the breezy
nights we whispered love

always, our voices always softer,
voice promising itself to voice
while we lay apart

in the grip of that force
that had fused us
so that nothing came between us.

EVERGREEN IN SUMMER

She was naked
except for a line of dirt
under her little fingernail.
The pool she swam in
still trembled slightly.
An owl called
in daylight, then another.
We were in the spruce forest.
From under her
I saw a white cloud
between her neck and shoulder.
I closed my eyes.
When I looked again
the sky was empty.
Brown needles clung
to the lines of my palm.

A MIRROR ON THE CAPE

Who loved us, who left us,
who mocked and scorned us,
who sent us the huge bouquet
with the minute whizzing bee,

who caressed us in a long dream
from which we woke
to the faint whoosh of breakers?

Who stole our car keys
and poured us black wine
in a cloudy glass?

We dressed in a daze.
That room was perfectly empty
except for a stain on a blue sheet,
our marriage, and the clamor of the ocean.

BUSHWICK: LATEX FLAT

Sadness of just-painted rooms.
We clean our tools
meticulously, as if currying horses:
the little nervous sash brush
to be combed and primped,
the fat old four-inchers
that lap up space
to be wrapped and groomed,
the ceiling rollers,
the little pencils
that cover nailheads
with oak gloss,
to be counted and packed:
camped on our dropsheets
we stare across gleaming floors
at the door and beyond it
the old city full of old rumors
of conspiracies, gunshots, market crashes:
with a little mallet
we tap our lids closed,
holding our breath, holding our lives
in suspension for a moment:
an extra drop will ruin everything.

THE PORTRAIT

My pregnant wife
is drawing in the front room.
Her soft lead
scritches faintly.
I'm in the work room
watching snow fall:
magnolia holds emptiness.
She tiptoes in and selects
dressed pine for her frame.
Alternate with the hammer,
a small exact silence
falls and rises.
Then the scrape
of Holland paper, and she
will come kiss me,
the wood dust
fine on her hand
where the ring is
already too tight.

THE BIRTH ROOM

We stare together
at the same fixed point
where there would be a curtain
if there were a window.
We try to breathe in time.

There is a method
to standing pain.
It's breaking down.

I don't suffer.
Still I'm amazed
how soon I'm overwhelmed.

In five minutes
we can call the doctor.

The lamp is dazzling
but there's no clock,
no lock, no mirror.

I keep winding a watch.
The second hand won't move.

A glass of water clouds
where you sipped it
a second, an hour ago.

When the nurse enters
with the stethoscope

44

it's as if we never doubted
and we hear the heartbeat—

command after command
in an unknown language,
directing us to be happy,
to be mother and father,
to grow old, to be loved,

to wait all our lives
for a single moment.

ONLY CHILD

1

I cradled my newborn daughter
and felt the heartbeat
pull me out of shock.
She didn't know
what her hands were:
she folded them. I asked her
was there a place
where there was no world.
She didn't know
what a voice was: her lips
were the shape of a nipple.

2

In the park the child says:
Watch me. It will not count
unless you see. And she shows me
the cartwheel, the skip, the tumble,
the tricks performed at leisure in midair,
each unknown until it is finished.
At home she orders:
see me eat. I watch her
curl on herself, sleep;
as I try to leave the dark room
her dreaming voice commands me: watch.

3

Always we passed the seesaw
on the way to the swings
but tonight I remember
the principle of the lever,
I sit the child at one end,
I sit near the center,
the fulcrum, at once she has power
to lift me off the earth
and keep me suspended
by her tiny weight, she laughing,
I stunned at the power of the formula.

LITTLE FALLS

My child cries in sleep.
I answer with her name.
I tell her who I am.
I remind her how we came here,
up Plank Road in the fog,
ragweed skittering
on the DeSoto panels,
how we laid the fire,
how we swapped stories
from deeper in childhood
while the eyes of a fox
watched us from nowhere.
She calms without waking.
Her breath is strong and steady.
If she calls again
it's from a fortunate dream
and I can't answer.

AUGUST HORIZON

The canoe picks up speed
and forges north with the weight
of our bodies and the thwarts
and the folded tent
and the ash paddles, the prow
cuts its notch in the sky
and my daughter points to the riverbank
and says "house," "tree," "bird,"
though she never used the words before
she pronounces them calmly
as if they were always there,
on shore: here at Little Falls
the stars bend with the J-stroke,
the dipper becomes a funnel, the plough
a jackknife, and when the moon rises
in a new part of the forest
abolishing all degrees of shadow
the child says "night."

IMMENSE FIRES AND NOT YET SUMMER

The face responsible for opinions
hasn't slept in three days,
the mouth in charge of facts
has begun to stutter.
The cloud that hides that city
is radiant and lights the room
where we watch, legs dangling
on the edge of an unmade bed.
I turn to tell you
"I foresaw this, so did you,
seeing this coming made us a couple."
Your finger is on your lips.
Your eyes are rapt, flares in reflection
cross your cheek like moods.
On the screen the armored personnel carriers
have arrived, already the shots sound
a split-second delayed, on a separate tape.

PART THREE

CROSSING THE ARK MOUNTAINS

Our map showed a straight line
to Hebron but the road forked
again and again with no sign,
sometimes a branch twisted back
to indicate a favorable direction,
sometimes only the gleam of aspen.
We kept climbing. Again and again
the spruce wall opened on a wider horizon,
a sparser foreground, a greater remove
from the tiny ruled fields.
The moon rose and at last
I stopped for directions at a farm.
I stepped over a child's toys,
a dry wading pool, a rope coil,
finding the glint in the goldenrod
where bodies had passed.
I came to the open door and knocked
gently, not to close it.
A blind dog came padding
to lick my hand in silence.
I thought I heard the squeak
of a cradle being rocked
and the hum of wasps.
At last I turned and the dog
sighed heavily and thumped down.
I walked back careful
of the doll's shoes soaked with rain,
the wheels, the spokes, the wagon.
You were waiting in the car,
your face streaked with tears.
Was it the evening in my eyes

that made you turn away?
We kept climbing and I was angry
that I could not give you happiness,
could not bring you the promise
of the valley where lights
had begun to flicker, a lamp,
high beams, the invisible windows
kindling one by one, pinpricks
into a world of pure fire.

THE LATCH

A dog barked at me
from behind the dingy white fence.
I glimpsed its flashing teeth,
dull white like surf.
It threw its body against the slats
in play or rage. I rang again.
Lights kindled in a high window.
A man with my face
came out buttoning his shirt
sleepily. He shone his flashlight
straight at the gate,
then to the right and left of me,
then in the trees.
My wife appeared beside him
with our child in her arms.
She, too, looked up
at the tossing elms, heavy with south wind,
swinging like bells, but with no noise
except twigs splintering.
The dog hurled itself
again and again, like a die cast,
the child stared straight at me
crying in silence, lips framing
my name, my father's name, the word
Father. Then the rain came.
They called the dog
and it went to them
tail tucked, the door closed,
the green curtain cinched shut
on nothing, but I stayed
at the gate, my right hand

on the oiled latch.
Sometimes a car passed
and the light enveloped my body
like a caress, knowing me,
gone, and I knelt
to fix an imaginary lace
or grope for a coin
I might have dropped
if I were still waiting.

THE GREAT GIFTS

I thought I'd love you
all my life
but you said no,
my love had fallen short,
I hadn't given you
the great gifts:

I wasted our treasure
on whims, on strangers:

as you spoke
you turned out the collar
of the coat you were packing
and smoothed the lapels
and motioned away
the almost-invisible fly
that had circled our bed
since the bill of divorcement.

Occasionally you glanced
sidelong at your watch.

From now on all the seconds
would be brutally precious.

FIRST GRADE HOMEWORK

The child's assignment:
"What is a city?"
All dusk she sucks her pencil
while cars swish by
like ghosts, neighbors' radios
forecast rain, high clouds,
diminishing winds: at last
she writes: "The city is everyone."
    Now it's time
for math, borrowing and exchanging,
the long discipleship
to zero, the stranger,
the force that makes us
what we study: father and child,
writing in separate books,
infinite and alone.

THE SCREEN

Every night in the narrow apartment
the child asks: what shall I do?
She's allowed television
as long as it's a nature picture
and I settle beside her and watch
the extinction of the mauritian kestrel,
the crested baboon, the great auk, extinction
beginning among the monkeys and flies,
but I stare at her small face rapt,
unbelievably hard in its mask
of pure attention: when the show is over
it will be time for night books,
the long file of words spoken softer
and softer, fainter than breath.

THE LAST BORDER

The child opens a brassbound album and asks:
"Are your parents or the pictures dead?
If they're not alive why do they have faces?"
To distract her, I point out the background:
oaks glinting in the twilight
and a road leading there. I tell her:
"That's a grove, perhaps they were resting
in the shade at the center
and that's why their faces
look so blurred; there's a donkey
grazing on grass from before the war,
a crow on a fence, if you look closely
you can see the sentry-box they'll pass
to cross the bridge, and if you could read
the labels on their bag would tell you
they've finally arrived at Olmos,
it's 1939, they may escape . . ."

THE LAST NIGHT OF EXILE

1 *The North*

As my daughter watches
I hammer in a picture
of the snowfields of Estonia.
While I sit resting
she comes with her pretend hammer
and tacks up an imaginary landscape
and straightens it, and admires
the smooth blank wall.

2 *Newborn*

My child says, of all things
what she most wants
is to be newborn,
a life measured
in hiccups, to have me

leaning over her crib
singing to her
and not know me.

THE OPPONENT

In the dark room
the child tosses her ball,
her small voice
counting the times
she can catch it in a row
safely . . . she mutters
Zero, the ball careens loose,
free of my care,
and she begins again.
I wonder what barrier
could she break
that would free her
of Zero—a thousand,
a hundred thousand?
The room fills with sun.
I dress in a trance.
She's lying asleep
late for school,
her homework blank,
her stuffed bears thrown
into corners of the room,
but the ball is safe
in her dreaming hand.

LEAVING LITTLE FALLS

When the last silo dipped
below the horizon, we pulled over
to check our route. But our map
was frayed, and cinched and buckled
in the space between knees and dashboard,
describing a world that meets itself
at center and corners. Spilt coffee
had incised frontiers, a cigarette burn
marked the county seat of emptiness.
We'd come back once too often
though the wheat was unchanged,
bowing in its inhuman richness.

PLUMS

My mother lay at St. Luke's
after the first stroke.
The doctor had ordered:
don't move a muscle.
Her eyes followed me.
If she craned her neck
it was against her will.

A voice behind a curtain
giggled and screamed.
My mother said:
That one's been crying
for nineteen years.
To heal I must believe;
now I have to hear that noise
night and day and be whole.

She said:
Since it's given to you,
part the drapes and look.
An old man sat in diapers,
his eyes blue-rimmed
with the cloudy authority
of a newborn, cheeks smooth.
He smiled again and again,
the light of recognition
kindling and diminishing.
I nodded and nodded.

I'd brought my mother supper—
diced lamb and spinach

cooked in her kitchen.
I fed her until she was satisfied
and ate the rest myself.
The portion I'd tried to make tiny
once again proved huge.

For dessert I'd made plum jelly.
We shared a plastic spoon,
savoring the tartness
and the sweetness,
each speaking shyly
of the record snows, each
listening only for that voice.

RETURNING TO THE CAPITAL

I was confused by the beggars—
there were none in our marriage
but now they thronged the station,
elbowing each other aside
as commuters do, each displaying
a scar, a metal leg,
a cancerous lip, or if whole
showing an immense sadness,
a rootlessness, an incoherence
stunning as a missing hand.
Like the other travelers
I thought it was a test of judgment.
I struggled to decipher
which wounds were cosmetic,
if satisfied I gave a coin
so long as I had change.
But when I came to our street
the beggars were younger,
a girl and her gaunt baby,
a boy who showed me
stumps from a war
I couldn't remember.
I pressed your bell,
a child's empty hand
still reaching out to me,
and your voice from long ago,
from childhood, called
"Who is it?" then shouted
"Who is it?"

THE HOTEL METROPOLE

I went knocking from door to door,
desperate to resume an old argument.

In one room an old man in an undershirt
was ironing a black serge suit.
He looked up, blinking.

Next door, an old woman
sat curling her sparse hair
with tongs and a dish of vinegar.

The higher doors did not open.

I wanted to tell you
how cruel you are,
how you locked me out of my life.

At last I had the proof.
Six buttons and a plum stone.

A picture of you in a satin dress
tied with a great black bow.

Your mother beside you
pursed her lips, cynical,
a face I might still find

behind the fire door
or if I broke the glass cabinet
where the hose of dust lies coiled.

RENDEZVOUS IN PROVIDENCE

Perhaps the gods are like us:
a couple breathless on a narrow bed.

They speak in low voices,
watching a fly cross the ceiling.

The self they lost comes back
on the breeze from a rickety fan.

A clock strikes. One touches
the other gently on the wrist.

As they undressed each other
now they dress themselves

in deep silence, and leave us
alone with this clock and mirror,

this love, this fear, these white hairs
tangled in a single comb.

NIGHT WALK IN PRADES

On a back road I stumbled
in frozen ruts, my hand
outstretched to parry
the absence of jack pine.

Then the fragmented stars
became whole—I'd crossed
into tilled land:

a leafless orchard:
on the smallest tree
a swing dangling
almost to the sparkling ground:

I'd come to the owner's house.
In his lit window
I saw a row of books:
for a long time I waited
for a hand to appear
and choose one title or another

—as if the dark were a mind
and had fashioned my body
only as a model
for my radiant cloud of breath.

THE MASTER SURGEON

I had arranged to meet you
in an alcove at St. Luke's
to discuss my symptoms.
The idea was: if I understood
the cause, I would be free.
I kept glancing at my watch
too quickly, scared to miss you.
I hadn't confirmed—perhaps
I'd asked too circumspectly,
not wanting to oblige,
and you'd taken my request
as an anecdote or parable.
I wrote out a dozen symptoms,
then crumpled the list
and recited it from memory,
surprised how the numbers
shaped and limited my fear.
At the appointed time, the faces
in the hall seemed so radiant
I could hardly glance at them:
an hour later, the passersby
were ordinary, etched like types:
an old woman with meaty arms
muttering, telling a rosary;
a guard whistling; an orderly
with a tic; a serene young bride.
Their faces reflected the lateness,
the harsh light, the halo of fatigue
you would have seen around me.
        Then you passed.
You were holding a child's hand,

talking to him passionately.
Hooked to a catheter,
he trundled a bag of urine.
You shortened your stride
with a visible effort.
Your face was averted
but I saw your happiness in his.
You motioned him to a door
I had never noticed,
set into the paneling.
It closed behind you.
I thought I saw gauges
and a tracheotomy hose.
I waited then for time itself,
for the softly humming clock
to click from minute to minute,
for the next sugary chord
in the bland constant music,
knowing at last I had power,
if not to heal, at least
to stand my ground.

THE THREAD OF THE CONVERSATION

You must have traveled through this city
before dawn, braving the cold and the addicts,
you must have bribed the guards
or posed as a surgeon on a mission,
and now you napped beside me in a metal chair.
I couldn't take my eyes off you
for fear you might be a dream.
I sensed dawn in the pallor of the screens.
I tried to remember how our last conversation ended
so we might pick up the thread—
I hadn't seen you in forty years
and in those days you were still my father.
We might have been speaking of pain,
of the mysteries of those thousand faces,
closer in darkness than in daylight
and all interchangeable, though some
express shock and others hope.
Perhaps we sat as we do now, one dreaming,
the other waiting, listening to the faint sirens,
the city's quarrels magnified by snow,
clatter of the night-shift leaving,
clash of bedpans in the corridor
where every door opens inwards.

FEVER IN A RENTED ROOM

I have to master this weakness
as a child learns
its mother's language.

Then each silence
becomes a signal:

the smoke in the window
bowing to a wind
I cannot feel,

the book in my lap
whose words swarm like bees,

the cup I can't lift
until it's empty.

THE BOND

You were the only one in that room
who was dead, the only one
with no hope of return,
and I gravitated to you
steadily, negotiating brief conversations
with the drunk sculptor
and the exhausted dancer:
but I was shy in your presence
and chattered about my prospects—
the vanities I'd hated in others.
You were calm and thoughtful,
peeling an orange as you listened,
wincing as the acid bit under your nails,
nodding eagerly when I paused.
You deplored the great rains
that had drowned the winter wheat.
I countered with my list of sacrifices
as if I could bind you to life
by suffering, and you frowned,
you put your hand on mine.
I could barely hear your answer—
I had to read your lips
with that music pounding
in your ears and mine—
but you comforted me, explaining
the power of detachment.
Lowering your eyes, you urged me
to teach myself patience,
to sleep more, to trade wine for milk,
to take care when I left,

given the lateness
and the difficulty of knowing
who rules these half-lit streets.

ABOUT THE AUTHOR

D. Nurkse's previous books of poetry include *Leaving Xaia, Voices Over Water, Staggered Lights, Shadow Wars,* and *Isolation in Action.* He has received two National Endowment for the Arts fellowships, the Whiting Writers' Award, the 1998 Bess Hokin Prize from *Poetry,* and a New York State Foundation for the Arts fellowship. In 2000, he received an Artist's Fund grant from the New York State Foundation for the Arts, and a Tanne Foundation grant. In 1996, he was appointed Poet Laureate of Brooklyn. He has also written widely on human rights.